HOW FIRM A FOUNDATION!

Where your Bible came from

How you got it

Why you should trust it

■

KENT RAMLER & RANDY LEEDY

BIBLE
MODULAR
SERIES

Bob Jones University Press, Greenville, South Carolina 29614

This textbook was written by members of the faculty and staff of Bob Jones University. Standing for the "old-time religion" and the absolute authority of the Bible since 1927, Bob Jones University is the world's leading Fundamentalist Christian university. The staff of the University is devoted to educating Christian men and women to be servants of Jesus Christ in all walks of life.

Providing unparalleled academic excellence, Bob Jones University prepares its students through its offering of over one hundred majors, while its fervent spiritual emphasis prepares their minds and hearts for service and devotion to the Lord Jesus Christ.

If you would like more information about the spiritual and academic opportunities available at Bob Jones University, please call **1-800-BJ-AND-ME** (1-800-252-6363). www.bju.edu

NOTE:
The fact that materials produced by other publishers may be referred to in this volume does not constitute an endorsement by Bob Jones University Press of the content or theological position of materials produced by such publishers. The position of Bob Jones University Press, and the University itself, is well known. Any references and ancillary materials are listed as an aid to the student or the teacher and in an attempt to maintain the accepted academic standards of the publishing industry.

How Firm a Foundation!

Kent Ramler, M.A. and Randy Leedy, Ph.D.
with Bryan Smith, M.A.

©1995, 1999 Bob Jones University Press
Greenville, South Carolina 29614

Printed in the United States of America
All rights reserved

ISBN 1-57924-265-0

15   14   13   12   11   10   9   8   7   6   5   4   3

CONTENTS

The Bible Stands

*he Bible stands like a rock undaunted
Mid the raging storms of time;
Its pages burn with the truth eternal,
And they glow with a light sublime.*

*The Bible stands though the hills may tumble,
It will firmly stand when the earth shall crumble;
I will plant my feet on its firm foundation,
For the Bible stands.*

*The Bible stands like a mountain tow'ring
Far above the works of men;
Its truth by none ever was refuted,
And destroy it they never can.*

*The Bible stands, and it will forever,
When the world has passed away;
By inspiration it has been given—
All its precepts I will obey.*

CHAPTER ONE

How Can You Know the Bible Is True?

①

Memory Verses: II Timothy 3:16 / II Peter 1:20-21

What Would *You* Say?

I'll never forget one summer night several years ago; I was sitting in my aunt's living room when she turned to me and innocently asked a few simple questions. "Kent," she said, "aren't you a Christian?"

Several other unsaved relatives in the room stopped what they were doing and listened with interest. After I replied that I was, she asked me how I knew that Christians were right and everybody else in the world was wrong. Why was I so sure that my religion was true? As an eighth grader, I began to feel the eyes of everyone in the room boring into me. Perhaps their eternal destinies would depend on how well I could defend what I believed. After thinking for a moment, I responded that my religion believed what the Bible said. "But how do you know the Bible is right?" she countered.

Here was another basic question that for me was an extremely difficult one to answer. I mumbled a few things, and mercifully the questioning stopped. I don't remember what I mumbled, but I do remember feeling very stupid and wondering to myself whether the Bible could be completely trustworthy. Could I stake my present life and eternal destiny on a book that billions of people did not believe?

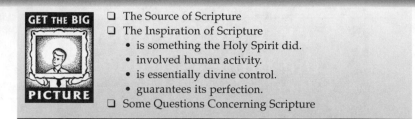

Years later I was traveling in the Chicago area with a youth evangelistic team. One night during the preaching, several teen guys slipped out the back and headed for the parking lot. Before they could reach their cars, I caught up to one guy named Bill (the name has been changed) and asked why he was leaving. He replied that his mom wanted him home before dark. It was 8:00 P.M., and the 17-year-old's appearance suggested that he was *not* the type to care about pleasing his parents. His excuse was lame to say the least. Bill proceeded to tell me that he did not believe the Bible but trusted in his own mind to determine his destiny. I asked him how he knew his opinion was true as opposed to the billions of other people who have opinions in the world. He shot back with, "How do you know that your opinion is true?" I told him that my opinion was based on the Bible and guaranteed to be true. If Bill had been inclined to continue the conversation, he would almost certainly have demanded how I could be so sure that *the Bible* is true.

> **Test Yourself!**
>
> Which challenge could you meet more quickly?
> - • "Give me two good reasons to trust the Bible."
> - • "Give me two good reasons you should have the car tonight."
>
> What does your answer tell you about yourself and your priorities?

No Christian can avoid this question. Your decisions throughout life will reflect what you believe about the Bible, and your faith in the Bible's trustworthiness will be challenged constantly as you witness for Christ. The main thrust of this course will be to explore this question. As so often happens, we will find that trying to answer one question raises more questions, and we will deal with these related questions as well. Your search will not be fruitless; in the end you will have excellent reasons for accepting the Bible as God's Word and for proclaiming it as such to others.

What the Bible Says About Itself

Our question, you remember, is "How do we know that the Bible is true?" This is not a special question that applies only to the Bible. We are bombarded daily with information clamoring for our attention and acceptance, and a wise person evaluates information before believing it. These evaluations always start with the source of the information. The trustworthiness of the information is directly related to the trustworthiness of the source. I told Bill that the Bible is guaranteed to be true because it came from God, and He makes no mistakes.

But this claim leads to another question: "How do we know that the Bible came from God?" Think for a moment about how we know where ordinary books come from. If your literature teacher asked you who wrote *Romeo and Juliet,* you would answer, "Shakespeare." Suppose she asked you how you knew that. Perhaps you would say you knew it because his name is on the title page as the author. But suppose she pressed you further and asked how you could know for sure that Shakespeare didn't steal *Romeo and Juliet* (or for that matter all his other plays) from some other writer, publishing them under his own name. About the only reasonable answer you could offer is that Shakespeare claimed to be the author, the people of his day accepted his claim, and you have no reason for claiming otherwise. Indeed, most authors take credit for their writings, and the writings themselves often contain further information about their origin. The author expects the reader to take his word for these things, and the reader seldom has reason to doubt them.

3

Think About It!

Which would you believe? Why or why not?
- a street peddler's story about where he got a watch he's trying to sell you
- a mechanic's explanation of why your car needs a new transmission
- the instructions for programming your VCR
- a politician's promise to lower your taxes

Any discussion about a book's origin, then, must begin with the author's own claims. Now, what happens when we bring this line of reasoning to the Bible? Does the Bible make any claims about its own origin? Obviously, the author's name is not printed on the cover. But the Bible asserts repeatedly that its ultimate author is God. In fact, more than thirty-eight hundred times the Old Testament uses language such as, "Thus saith the Lord" and "The word of the Lord came," claiming divine origin for what is written. If you set out to discover where the Bible came from, then you will soon find that the Book itself claims to have come from God. Your only reasonable choice is to accept this claim unless you can prove it false.

There have been many attempts to prove the Bible false, and we will eventually look at some of them. For now, though, we will confine ourselves to the question of what the Bible says about itself. Let's start with II Timothy 3:16: "All scripture is given by inspiration of God, and is profitable." This verse teaches clearly that the Bible came from God. But how did God "write" the Bible? With the exception of the Ten Commandments, no one has ever had God's Word in God's own handwriting! Instead, God prompted men to write His Word, and He helped them to write it accurately. This verse uses the word *inspiration* to describe God's activity in giving us His Word. What does the word mean? Furthermore, what really is *Scripture?* We say we believe that verse, but what does it mean?

The Meaning of Inspiration

For the remainder of this lesson, let's tackle the first of these questions, discussing what *inspiration* means and what the Bible says about the subject. What does it mean? In this verse the words "given by inspiration of God" come from one Greek word that

Scripture? Inspiration?

literally means "God-breathed." Does this answer your question? Probably not. Here is a definition paraphrased from Louis Gaussen, a well-known scholar on the subject. Inspiration is the process by which the Holy Spirit guided the Scripture writers so that their words were the very words God wanted written, with nothing added, omitted, or mistaken.

Inspiration is something the Holy Spirit did.

Let's examine this definition to be sure you understand its most important points. From the outset, we must realize that inspiration is a work of God. More specifically, it is a work of the Holy Spirit.

How do we know this is true? Many New Testament passages clearly refer to the working of the Holy Spirit in the writing of the Old Testament passages that they quote (Mark 12:36; Heb. 3:7). Second Peter 1:21 states that the Old Testament writers were "moved by the Holy Ghost." Second Timothy implies this by saying that Scripture is "God-breathed."

Inspiration involves human activity.

Second, our definition of inspiration points out that men were involved in the process. Notice that II Peter 1:21 refers to both divine and human activity: "*men . . . spake as they were moved by the Holy Ghost.*" The Bible did not just miraculously appear; God used *men* to do the actual writing. Thus Paul can call attention to his personal activity in writing the book of Galatians, saying in 6:11, "Ye see how large a letter I have written unto you with mine own hand."

Inspiration is essentially divine control.

It is easy enough to understand that both God and men were involved in the writing of the Bible. This third point of the definition is where matters become more difficult. How, exactly, did

Some people argue that, while the Bible is a very good book, it is not the Word of God. But if you think about it, you will realize that it is impossible to view the Bible this way without contradicting yourself.

Repeatedly, and in many different ways, the Bible claims to have come from God. If it did not come from God, then those claims are false, and the Bible contains many lies. A book full of lies is not a good book.

If the Bible is a good book at all, it must be God's Book as well.

God and men work together? Was it simply a joint venture between equal partners? What was happening between God and men in the writing of the Scripture? These questions lead us to consider what *inspiration* really means. You know what it means to sleep, to run, to think, and to laugh, for example, but can you explain what it means *to inspire* in the sense we're discussing?

Again II Peter 1:21 gives important information by saying that the Holy Spirit "moved" the human writers. We can understand the meaning of the word *moved* more clearly if we look to Acts 27:15 for an illustration. In that passage, Paul is traveling to Rome in a grain ship. A violent storm catches the ship, and the sailors can do nothing but surrender, letting the wind determine the ship's course. The Greek

word translated "let her drive" in Acts 27:15 is the same verb translated "moved" in II Peter 1:21. Just as the wind was totally in control of the ship's destination, the Holy Spirit controlled the whole process of writing Scripture. This is the basic meaning of *inspiration:* God's control over the human writing process.

No doubt you've figured out that we are using *inspire* in a different sense than you're accustomed to. As a theological term, the word does not mean the same thing as, for example, a coach's inspiring his team to play well or a poet's being inspired to write beautifully. In this course, the word has nothing to do with feelings or motivation; it refers simply to God's giving His Word in the Bible.

No one fully understands the exact nature of this control or the extent to which it reached. Some theologians believe that the human authors were like secretaries simply taking dictation. Others teach that God controlled the human authors' upbringing, education, and spiritual experience so that they could express God's truth through their own personalities. While this latter view accounts for differences in writing style from one writer to another, it does not deny the fact that the Holy Spirit ultimately controlled the writing process, keeping the human authors from making mistakes. When we learn the full truth in heaven, we probably will find that it is some combination of these views.

Inspiration guarantees perfection.

The fourth important point contained in our definition of *inspiration* is the fact that inspiration results in a Bible that contains no error. (The term used by theologians to refer to the absence of error in the Bible is *inerrancy.*) This belief in inerrancy is a subject of great debate in Christian circles today. Theological liberals (those who reject fundamental doctrines of the Bible such as Creation, the virgin birth of Christ, etc.) view the Bible as human literature that has, at best, slightly more of the truth of God in it than other literature. They think the writers were as prone to error as the writers of any other books. Liberals simply choose what they think is good in the Bible and ignore the rest.

On the conservative side of theology, there is widespread acceptance of the Bible as unique literature with God as its author in some sense. But even many of these people restrict the Bible's inerrancy to its teaching on moral issues, allowing for errors in matters of science, history, and geography. We will soon see, though, that this position is not acceptable. Traditional, orthodox Christianity over the centuries has maintained a firm belief in what theologians call *verbal inspiration.* This simply means that *every word* of Scripture is inspired and without error.

Let's look at some examples proving that Jesus and the apostles considered previously written Scripture as perfect. In Galatians 3:16 Paul builds his argument based on the singular "seed" (referring to the promise made to Abraham in Gen. 22:18)

The fact that different writing styles are apparent throughout the Bible has been taken by some to prove that the human writers chose their own words under the Spirit's guidance. Others, however, maintain that the Holy Spirit chose the words for them, reflecting what He knew to be their personal style. Differences in style are an undeniable fact, but that fact ultimately proves nothing about the degree to which the writers' human personalities were active within the process of inspiration.

Can you think of any reasons that you would expect Paul, for instance, to write in a style different from John?

as opposed to the plural "seeds." Christ argues that the Old Testament teaches the doctrine of the resurrection (which some of His hearers did not believe) based on the present tense of the verb "I am" (Matt. 22:32; Exod. 3:6). Scripture clearly views inspiration as applying to words and verb tenses. God cannot make mistakes; therefore, His Word cannot have errors in it.

But, But, But . . .

But wait a minute. Doesn't Paul's reference to "all scripture" in II Timothy 3:16 mean specifically the Old Testament? And certainly II Peter 1:20-21 ("For the *prophecy* came not *in old time* by the will of man . . .) refers just to the Old Testament. Furthermore, those thirty-eight hundred instances where "Thus saith the Lord" is written are in the Old Testament. And when Jesus quoted and verified Scripture, the New Testament had not even been written. How then do we know that the New Testament is inspired on the same level as the Old?

The Teaching of the New Testament

These are good questions for which there are good answers. It is evident, for example, that Peter considered Paul's writings to be inspired. He implies in II Peter 3:15-16 that Paul's epistles were as authoritative as the Old Testament Scriptures. At the beginning of the same chapter, Peter equates the prophecy of the Old Testament with the commandments of the New Testament apostles. Furthermore, if you check the sources of Paul's quotations in I Timothy 5:18, you will discover that Paul put Luke's Gospel on a par with Deuteronomy. When we realize that the writings of the

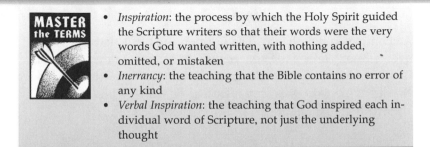

apostles (II Pet. 3:2), the epistles of Paul (II Pet. 3:16), and the Gospel of Luke (I Tim. 5:18) were all directly or indirectly pointed out as inspired, we can understand that claims of divine authorship apply to the New Testament as well as the Old.

The Aid of the Holy Spirit

We must deal with one more issue concerning the New Testament. These writings are based on three important foundations: the teachings of the Old Testament, the teachings and actions of Christ, and the truth of His death and resurrection. The second of these foundations required very accurate recall on the part of the apostles. How could men remember years later exactly what Christ had said and taught (the Gospel writers especially)? The first New Testament book was not written until fifteen years after Christ was gone. He died and rose again around A.D. 30. John did not write his Gospel until A.D. 85. That leaves more than fifty years between! Think back to a special speaker you heard perhaps as much as a year ago. Can you remember exactly, word for word, what he said? Of course not. Most people can't remember the sermon they heard last week.

The solution to this problem lies in some things Jesus said to the disciples in John 14 and 16. These chapters show the men in a state of discouragement because Jesus says He will be leaving them soon. To comfort them, He assures them that the Holy Spirit will be sent to bring all things to their remembrance (14:26). Later Jesus reassures them further by adding that the Holy Spirit will guide the disciples into all truth (John 16:12-13). Thus the Gospels are not exaggerated oral traditions passed down over the years until they were finally recorded. Neither are the Epistles a collection of "new truths" dreamed up by strange people with too much time on their hands. The Gospels are the actual words and events from Christ's life supernaturally brought to the writers' remembrance, and the Epistles contain the truth into which the Holy Spirit led the writers as they reflected on Christ's life, death, and resurrection.

Summary

We hope your understanding of inspiration is better now than it was when you began this lesson. Inspiration is a work of God through men controlled by the Holy Spirit, who insured that the writings are the very words that God intended, without error or omission.

Review Questions

1. When you evaluate the reliability of information you receive, the first thing you evaluate is the reliability of the

2. An investigation into the origin of an ordinary book begins with

3. In II Timothy 3:16, the words "given by inspiration of God" are the translation of a single Greek word that literally means

4. Which member of the Trinity was especially involved in the work of inspiration?

5. What verse teaches clearly that inspiration is essentially divine control?

6. The name of the doctrine that God inspired each word of the Bible is

7. Which epistle writer quoted from Luke's Gospel and placed it on a par with Deuteronomy?

8. Explain how the writers of the Gospels were able to recall the very words of Jesus with complete accuracy.

_____9. Jesus' teachings did not touch upon the doctrine of inerrancy.

_____10. Paul used the term *Scripture* to describe Peter's writings.

_____11. Which of the following statements is most precise?

    A. God wrote the Bible.

    B. Men wrote the Bible.

    C. Both A and B are true.

    D. The Bible is still in the process of being written.

_____12. Identify the theological danger in the statement "The Bible contains the Word of God."

    A. It does not explain the meaning of the Bible.

    B. It allows the possibility that some things in the Bible are not God's Word.

    C. It does not specifically describe the Holy Spirit's role in inspiration.

    D. It implies that only the Bible is God's Word.

_____13. Inspiration and inerrancy are foundational doctrines because

    A. the trustworthiness of all other doctrines depends upon them.

    B. Paul said they are the most important doctrines.

    C. they are the first things Jesus taught His disciples.

    D. they are accepted by all professing Christians, whether liberal or conservative.

The following statements are actual published definitions of the term *inspiration*. Match each definition with the description that fits it best. One description will be used twice.

A. good definition   B. weak on inerrancy   C. unacceptable

____14. A work of the Holy Spirit, causing His energies to flow into the spontaneous exercises of the writers' faculties, elevating and directing where need be, and everywhere securing the errorless expression in language of the thought designed by God.

____15. Inspiration is that influence of the Spirit of God upon the minds of the Scripture writers which made their writings the record of a progressive divine revelation, sufficient, when taken together and interpreted by the same Spirit who inspired them, to lead every honest inquirer to Christ and to salvation.

____16. We call our Bible inspired, by which we mean that by reading and studying it we find our way to God, we find His will for us, and we find how we can conform ourselves to His will.

____17. Inspiration is that inexplicable power which the Divine Spirit put forth of old on the authors of holy Scripture, in order to guide them even in the employment of the words they used, and to preserve them alike from all error and from all omission.

18. A publisher's blurb for *The Greatest Story Ever Told,* by Fulton Oursler, contains the following statement: "Originally written in 1949, the book has been acclaimed by the clergy of all faiths for its inspiration and authenticity!" Explain the difference between the meaning of inspiration in the advertisement and its meaning in this lesson. Did the publisher commit a sin by calling the book inspired? Why or why not?

19. Evaluate the following definition in light of this lesson's teaching on the meaning of inspiration: "Inspiration is that influence of the Spirit of God upon the minds of the Scripture writers which made their writings the record of a progressive divine revelation, sufficient, when taken together and interpreted by the same Spirit who inspired them, to lead every honest inquirer to Christ and to salvation." (A. H. Strong)

20. Evaluate the following definition in light of this lesson's teaching on the meaning of inspiration: "We call our Bible inspired, by which we mean that by reading and studying it we find our way to God, we find his will for us, and we find how we can conform ourselves to his will." (Robert Horton)

21. Evaluate the following definition in light of this lesson's teaching on the meaning of inspiration: "A work of the Holy Spirit, causing His energies to flow into the spontaneous exercises of the writers' faculties, elevating and directing where need be, and everywhere securing the errorless expression in language of the thought designed by God." (B. B. Warfield)

22. Explain how the description of a ship caught in a storm (Acts 27:15) contributes to our understanding of the meaning of inspiration.

CHAPTER TWO

Which Books Belong in the Bible?

②

Memory Verses: Luke 24:44 / II Peter 3:2

A Tougher Question Yet

The previous lesson called attention to II Timothy 3:16, "All scripture is given by inspiration of God," and questioned the meaning of two terms: *inspiration* and *Scripture*. We have examined the meaning of the first term; now we must discuss the second. When we ask "What is *Scripture?*" what we are really asking is which

ancient writings deserve to be recognized as the authoritative Word of God.

Did you know that the sixty-six books of our Bible are not the only books written by God-fearing people during that period of history? The Bible itself refers to other written works from its own time period, such as the books of the chronicles of the kings of Israel and of Judah. How do we know that our Bible contains all the right books? Obviously, someone had to collect these

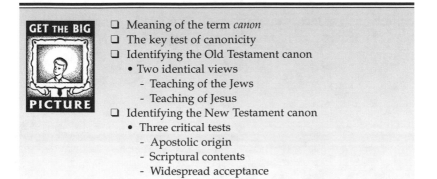

GET THE BIG PICTURE

- ❏ Meaning of the term *canon*
- ❏ The key test of canonicity
- ❏ Identifying the Old Testament canon
  - • Two identical views
    - - Teaching of the Jews
    - - Teaching of Jesus
- ❏ Identifying the New Testament canon
  - • Three critical tests
    - - Apostolic origin
    - - Scriptural contents
    - - Widespread acceptance

books, choosing to include the ones we have in the Bible and to reject the ones we don't. How do we know that they made the right decisions?

Perhaps you have never even thought of this question before. Admittedly, an unbeliever is not as likely to ask you this question as he is to ask the question Kent was asked by his aunt. Most people do not know enough about ancient literature to be aware of these other books. But if you make a habit of talking to people about the gospel, you will eventually face this question, and it will come probably from someone who is intelligent and well educated. There are good answers to this question, though they are not simple. We hope you will take the trouble to think this question through so that you can have the answers ready when you need them.

You Can't Shoot the Canon

Considering which books belong in the Bible deals with the topic of the "canon." The word *canon* (pronounced just like *cannon*) is the English spelling of a Greek word that means "straight rod," or "ruler," a device for measuring conformity to a standard. The canon of Scripture is the body of writings that measures up to the standard of divine inspiration and authority. A related word, *canonical* (accented on the second syllable), means "belonging to the canon." For example, the sixty-six books of the Bible are sometimes called the canonical books; other writings excluded from the canon are called noncanonical.

You should bear in mind that the noncanonical books are not entirely evil; indeed, you can benefit from reading them. But these books lack evidence of inspiration and therefore carry no binding authority.

Do you remember what we said in the previous lesson about examining a book's own claims about its origin? If you approach the noncanonical books this way, you will find that most of them do not claim to have come from God. But what about those that do? Can we disprove that claim? We can; the noncanonical books that claim divine origin contain such obvious errors that everyone who studies them recognizes their imperfections. Rather than focus on the excluded books, though, the rest of this lesson will examine the reasons for accepting the sixty-six books of our Bible as we have them.

The Bottom Line Up Front

I remember reading with some interest a publisher's preface to Alexander Dumas's *Three Musketeers*. Encouraging me to read widely, the publisher reasoned, "A book becomes a classic only when enough people over an extended period of time decide they like the book." Then he exhorted me to be an avid reader and share with others the books that I find especially enjoyable. Thus I would become part of the very important process of making classics.

However, the publisher failed to realize that I no more make a book a classic than a child makes his dad his dad just by calling him "Dad." If a little girl lovingly exclaims "Daddy" when her father comes, she is simply recognizing a pre-existing reality. So also, when a reader discovers the inherent "classic quality" of a book, he does not make the book a classic; he only confirms what is already true.

You Write the Book; We'll Make It a Classic!

Classics ᴙ R ᴙ Us

Boy, this is gonna take a lot of work!

That publisher's misconception is sadly common among students of the Bible. Many think that the sixty-six books of the Old and New Testaments became "the Bible" when the early church decided they should be. If that were so, the authority of these books would rest on man's opinion. In reality, the church simply recognized what was already true.

Christ told His contemporaries that His sheep have the ability to hear His voice and to avoid the voice of a "stranger" (John 10:2-5, 11, 27). For those early believers, as for us, the key test in determining canonicity was the testimony of the Holy Spirit in their hearts that the books were from God. Those that have a personal relationship with the author of Scripture hear the voice of God in the books He has written.

> *The key test of canonicity: the testimony of the Holy Spirit in heart of the believer that the books are from God.*

Some find this conclusion dissatisfying because it seems to make such an important decision entirely subjective. However, this God-chosen means of revealing which books are canonical is the ideal means. Think about it. If God had decided that *men* would identify which books are canonical by using their own system of tests, *men* would be standing in judgment over the text. However, neither God nor His Word will be judged by men. The Lord has initiated communication with man by producing a flawless text. Furthermore, He has commended that text to believers by placing in their hearts the same Spirit who wrote the Word. Thus the Word testifies to the Spirit in the believer's heart that it is from God. Not even when considering canonicity does man judge the text; rather, he is judged by it.

The rest of this lesson deals with various facts from history that demonstrate that the Holy Spirit has been confirming the divine origin of these sixty-six books in the hearts of His people for millenia. As you read through these observations, carefully consider how different these books are from all others.

The Old Testament

Since the Old and New Testaments represent different periods in the history of God's people, it is not surprising that the question of the canon involves somewhat different issues in each case. It will be easier, then, to discuss this question in two parts. Let's start with the Old Testament.

Which books belong in the Old Testament Scriptures? Traditionally, our Old Testament includes only thirty-nine books. Some groups (including the Roman Catholic Church) have insisted on including fourteen other books called the Apocrypha. Among the better known apocryphal books are I Maccabees, which contains fascinating accounts of the Jewish wars just before the time of Christ, and Bel and the Dragon, which adds information concerning the life of Daniel. None of the apocryphal books was written before 300 B.C., at least 100 years later than the last universally accepted book of the Old Testament. How should we view these books? Should we seriously consider them as Scripture?

The Jewish View of the Old Testament

Since before the time of Christ, the Jews have classified their scriptural books into three main divisions: the Law, the Prophets, and the Writings. The last of these divisions was sometimes called "the Psalms" because Psalms dominates that section. These divisions include the same thirty-nine books that we have in our Old Testament. The Jews, though, arranged them in a different order, beginning with Genesis and ending with II Chronicles. To us it

DID YOU KNOW?

One day Christopher Columbus picked up a book written by Pierre d'Ailly, a Catholic scholar. The author proposed that the earth was a sphere and that the distance from the western coast of Europe to the eastern coast of Asia could be sailed in only a few days. He based this estimate on a verse found in the Apocrypha of the Vulgate (the Catholic Bible in Latin). The verse states that God created the earth with six parts land and one part water (IV Esdras 6:42; non-Catholics call the book II Esdras).

This appeal to "the Bible" convinced Columbus. Although this misinformation led to the discovery of the Americas, it nearly cost Columbus his life.

seems odd to put II Chronicles last, because it does not cover the last period of Old Testament history. However, the Jews focused on the date of *writing*, and they believe that Ezra wrote II Chronicles as the last scriptural book around 424 B.C.

The writings of a man named Josephus confirm that the Jews had this view of the Old Testament canon. Writing shortly after A.D. 70, he states that every Jew believed that no more books were added to the Old Testament after Artaxerxes, a Persian king who died in 424 B.C. They believed further that no material was added to the thirty-nine accepted books.

Jesus' View of the Old Testament

Let's zero in now on why our thirty-nine books and no others are recognized as canonical. In Luke 11:37-52, Christ condemns the Jewish leaders for their hypocrisy, pronouncing them guilty of the blood of all the prophets from Abel to Zechariah. Why did Christ single out these two martyrs? When we identify these men more carefully, the answer becomes plain. It gets a bit compli-cated, but stay with us; we're going somewhere worthwhile.

Abel, of course, is the son of Adam who was murdered by his brother Cain in Genesis 4. But who is Zechariah? Jesus says the man was slain between the altar and the temple. This probably is not the Zechariah who wrote a book of the Bible, for we have no indication that he died as a martyr. Instead, the proper identifica-tion is the Zechariah who was killed in the temple area, by order of King Joash, as recorded in II Chronicles 24:20-21.

Now we're ready to see how these words from Jesus confirm the limitation of the Old Testament canon to thirty-nine books. Recall that in the Jewish Scriptures, Genesis is the first book and II Chronicles is the last. Christ was saying that the Pharisees were guilty of the blood of all the prophets from the beginning of the first book to the end of the last book. Another way of thinking of it is that Christ was including all the murdered prophets "from A to Z." By making no mention of the Apocrypha, Jesus puts a clear stamp of approval upon the Jewish canon of thirty-nine books.

The Law

Genesis, Exodus, Leviticus, Numbers, Deuteronomy

The Prophets

Former Prophets
Joshua, Judges, I & II Samuel, I & II Kings

Latter Prophets
Isaiah, Jeremiah, Ezekiel, Hosea, Joel, Amos, Obadiah, Jonah, Micah, Nahum, Habakkuk, Zephaniah, Haggai, Zechariah, Malachi

The Writings

Psalms, Job, Proverbs, Ruth, Song of Solomon, Ecclesiastes, Lamentations, Esther, Daniel, Ezra, Nehemiah, I & II Chronicles

Another evidence for the rejection of the Apocrypha as Scripture is found in Luke 24:44. "And he [Jesus] said unto them, These are the words which I spake unto you, while I was yet with you, that all things must be fulfilled, which were written in the law of Moses, and in the prophets, and in the psalms, concerning me." Notice the threefold division recognized by the Jews. Again Jesus excludes the Apocrypha even though it had existed for hundreds of years by this time.

As we have already indicated, the Jews accepted only the thirty-nine books of the Old Testament as canonical. Jesus, Himself a Jew, grew up with this teaching and knew that His audiences believed this. When Jesus taught concerning the Scripture, if He had wanted to include the Apocrypha as inspired, He would have had to deal specifically with the issue in order to correct the faulty thinking of His friends and listeners. He never did so. He allowed them to continue believing that the thirty-nine books they accepted as inspired were the only ones that belonged in the Old Testament.

The New Testament

Let's move on to the New Testament, which contains twenty-seven books of Scripture. Recently some unbelievers have renewed their efforts to omit certain books (such as Revelation) or portions (such as verses on hell) and to add books (such as the Gospel of Thomas). Such scattered challenges, however, should not disturb God's people, for the Holy Spirit continues to confirm the canonicity of these twenty-seven books alone. Nevertheless, in seeking a more detailed answer, we should consider the contributions of our spiritual forefathers. The early church, while facing challenges much greater than those just mentioned, developed several tests for recognizing which books belong in the New Testament. True believers since then have found these tests reassuring. they express concretely the "seal of approval" we all sense from God's Spirit.

Apostolic Origin

First, the early church concluded that each book had to be written by an apostle or by someone closely associated with an apostle. There is an important reason behind this test. Jesus made it clear that the apostles would be His representatives in founding the church and that their decisions would reflect God's truth and carry God's authority (John 14:26; Eph. 2:19-20; II Pet. 3:2). In a matter so crucial for the church as the writing of the New Testament, the apostles' role was vital. Furthermore, there is no biblical evidence that this divine sanction would carry on to succeeding generations of church leaders; the apostles were the *only* ones with such authority.

It was not necessary, though, for a book to have been actually *written* by an apostle. If a book originated in connection with an apostle's work, it could be assumed to carry the apostle's approval,

MASTER the TERMS

- **Canon**: the collection of books approved as meeting the standard of divine inspiration and authority
- **Scripture**: the sixty-six canonical books of the Old and New Testaments
- **Apocrypha**: Jewish and Christian works dated in or near biblical times but not accepted as canonical

even if someone else wrote it. For example, James, the half-brother of Jesus Christ, wrote his epistle about A.D. 48 in Jerusalem. He was not an apostle himself, but he lived among the apostles, associating closely with them. If the apostles had not considered the book to be Scripture, it would be difficult to account for its wide acceptance by the early church.

We need to consider one more point concerning this test of canonicity. The test of apostolic origin puts a limit on how long the canon remained open to new writings. John outlived the other apostles, and he died around A.D. 100. It stands to reason, then, that nothing written after that date can be considered apostolic.

Scriptural Contents

The second test involved an examination of the contents of the book. Obviously, no book containing errors or contradicting other Scripture could be viewed as canonical.

Widespread Acceptance

The third test laid down the requirement that a book must have enjoyed wide acceptance and use by the early church. If Buwanna,

Think About It!

There is an important difference between Luther's questions about the canon and those of modern skeptics. Luther was committed (and submitted!) to the Bible as the Word of God; he labored over which books deserved that recognition. Today's skeptics accept nothing as divinely inspired. Their goal is merely to point out some books as having exercised sufficient influence on Christianity to deserve inclusion in that religion's body of sacred literature. Between these points of view lies a difference as great as the difference between life and death.

a tribal chieftain in North Africa, had written a book, it probably would have been well received in his particular area, regardless of the value of its contents. After all, rejecting it would be hazardous to your health! But somebody in Rome or Ephesus who had never heard of this great tribal chieftain would pay it about as much attention as the average high-school student pays a grammar book—unless its contents commended it as helpful and trustworthy. This test assumes that anything *God* writes will commend itself to every soul energized by His Holy Spirit. A book lacking this widespread acceptance does not deserve recognition as the Word of God.

Conclusion

The Holy Spirit testifies to the authenticity of the books He has written. That testimony in the heart of believers is His "seal of approval." Is it possible that we have misunderstood that testimony? Hardly, for at every point in history when the question has come up and the evidence has been reviewed, the consensus of godly men and women concerning which books deserve a place in Scripture has consistently been the same. These books, and these alone, are inspired.

By now you should have a clear understanding of II Timothy 3:16, "All scripture is given by inspiration of God. . . ." The sixty-six books of our Bible, Genesis to Revelation, are the very words of God, written by men under His control, and free from all error.

Review Questions

1. What ancient author specifically described the Jews' beliefs regarding the Old Testament canon?

2. What is the "seal of approval" that God has put upon the inspired books?

_____3. The Bible refers to other books written during its own time.

_____4. Once settled by the early church, the canon never again became a controversial issue.

_____5. The Zechariah who was martyred wrote a book of the Bible.

_____6. The canon of Scripture is

   A. the dozen or so books of the Bible that contain the key doctrines of salvation.
   B. the body of doctrine clearly taught in all the books of the Bible.
   C. the collection of books that give clear evidence of divine inspiration.
   D. the early church's decision that the New Testament is equal in authority to the Old.

_____7. Which of the following is *not* one of the noncanonical books mentioned in this lesson?

   A. I Maccabees
   B. Bel and the Dragon
   C. The Testament of Hezekiah
   D. The Gospel of Thomas

_____8. Which of the following was *not* used by the Jews of Jesus' day to designate a major section of the Old Testament?

   A. The Law
   B. The Wisdom Books
   C. The Psalms
   D. The Prophets

_____9. Which of the following is *not* one of the criteria used to determine the canon of the New Testament?

   A. The book must contain Old Testament quotations.
   B. The book must have originated within the apostolic circle.
   C. The book must enjoy widespread acceptance.
   D. The book must not contradict scriptural teaching.

_____10. The noncanonical books

   A. have some value but no authority.
   B. are the only books that Roman Catholics accept as Scripture.
   C. were written by companions of the apostles.
   D. were specifically pointed out and rejected by Jesus.

_____11. The apocryphal books

   A. have never been printed as part of the Bible.
   B. were written by Roman Catholic monks.
   C. are biographies of early church leaders.
   D. contain both fact and fiction.

12. Explain the role of the apostles in determining which books
    are authoritative for the church. Is this role restricted to the
    New Testament writings? On what basis can a book not writ-
    ten by an apostle be considered apostolic? Name as many of
    these books as you can. What chronological limit does this
    test impose upon the New Testament canon?

13. Explain how Jesus' statement about the martyrs "from Abel to Zechariah" confirms the traditional Old Testament canon of thirty-nine books.

14. Explain the difference between Martin Luther's questions about the canon and the unbelief of modern critics.

15. Explain the key terms in this statement (the italicized words): "The *canon* of *Scripture* does not include the *Apocrypha*."

16. What is the key test of canonicity? Defend this test against its most obvious objection.

17. Suppose tomorrow's newspaper contains the surprising headline: "Long lost New Testament book found, author claims to be the Apostle Peter." Would you consider this book canonical? Why or why not?

CHAPTER THREE

Do You Have God's Word Today? *Part 1*

③

Memory Verses: I Peter 1:24, 25

Life Before Xerox

Imagine what life was like before someone invented the photocopier. Today, all you have to do to copy a document is find a copier, pay a small fee, and push a button. Instantly, your exact duplicate is ready. This process can sure help with library research! Even more amazing is the fact that you can get thousands of copies with little effort if you have access to a printing press and know how to use it. Modern technology has made it possible for us to enjoy more newspapers, magazines, documents, and books than any previous generation. As a result, mass production of written materials has become something taken for granted, and we can hardly imagine a time when the case was otherwise.

But the case certainly was otherwise when the Bible was written. Furthermore, for nearly fourteen hundred years after John finished the Book of Revelation, the only way to copy the Scripture

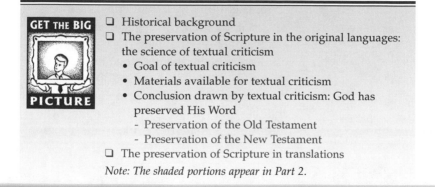

GET THE BIG PICTURE

❏ Historical background
❏ The preservation of Scripture in the original languages: the science of textual criticism
 • Goal of textual criticism
 • Materials available for textual criticism
 • Conclusion drawn by textual criticism: God has preserved His Word
  - Preservation of the Old Testament
  - Preservation of the New Testament
❏ The preservation of Scripture in translations
Note: The shaded portions appear in Part 2.

was to do it by hand. Do you suppose it would be humanly possible to copy the whole Bible without making a mistake? After all, if you're like most students, you sometimes have trouble even copying down your homework assignments correctly!

This lesson and the one following will explore some of the history and significance of the fact that for centuries the only way to reproduce the Bible was to copy it by hand. You probably thought the last lesson was a little more challenging than the first. These next two lessons will challenge you a little more yet. Perhaps it would be nice to leave out the hard things and stick to the simple. But people have a way of asking hard questions, and it is good for Christians to be able to answer them. In fact, you may have asked some of these questions yourself as you have worked your way through this book. So put your brain in gear and see what you can learn. We think you will be glad you did.

Facts and a Question

Let us put before you four historical facts and then raise an important question. The first fact is that God inspired every single word written down by the human authors of Scripture. The first lesson of this book established this crucial point of Christian doctrine. The second, third, and fourth facts are somewhat unsettling; they raise questions about whether God's Word has survived until today. The second fact is that the original documents of Scripture (called *autographs*) have disappeared. The third fact is that the handwritten copies (called *manuscripts*) by which the Bible has come to us over the centuries contain slightly different wording, and no manuscript is entirely free from copyists' errors. This is not a theory or a guess. Anyone who can read the original languages of Scripture can look at these manuscripts, or at reproductions of them, and see for himself that they occasionally differ from one another and that all evidence scribal mistakes. The fourth fact is that your Bible is a translation

*G*od inspired every word in the autographs.

*T*hese autographs have disappeared.

*N*o two existing manuscripts agree in every detail, and all contain some scribal errors.

*Y*our Bible is a translation from these manuscripts.

34

from ancient languages; not a single word God originally inspired was in English.

The question, then, is obvious. How can you know that you have the Word of God today? How can you be sure that God's Word has not been defiled by the human hands that have copied and recopied it or by those who have translated it into your language? Can you really be certain that the Bible you hold in your hands is the Word of God?

This question deals with the issue of the *preservation* of God's Word. We have maintained that God inspired the sixty-six books of our Bible so that every word of them is His Word. The questions we raise in this lesson deal with what God has done to preserve His Word so that it remains available in every generation.

The preservation of God's Word is an important issue. Unbelievers have often seized upon the differences among the manuscripts as a reason not to believe that God inspired the Bible. If we wish to maintain our position, we cannot stop with showing that God inspired the words originally written. We also must show that those words survive today.

We will divide our discussion into two sections. First we will deal with the preservation of God's Word in its original languages by the process of manuscript copying. Later we will take up the preservation of God's Word in other languages by the process of translation.

Copy All You Want!

Your first reaction to the idea of copying someone else's work is probably negative. It sounds like cheating. Remember, though, that in the ancient world, the kind of copying we are discussing was the equivalent of today's book publishing. It was more than an acceptable practice; it was a highly valued profession. The difference between "copying" then and now, of course, is that the ancient copyists were not representing the writings as their own; they were publishing the works of others.

The question we are dealing with is whether we can be sure that God's Word has survived intact over centuries and centuries of hand copying. If all the manuscripts were identical, there would be no question at all. But the manuscripts are not all the same, as we have observed. So how can we know that God's Word has been preserved for us in its original languages?

The first thing you need to realize about this question is that it involves issues that become quite complicated. The study of manuscript differences gets so complicated, in fact, that an entire field of scholarship has developed around it. Our purpose in discussing the issue with you is not to take you deep into these difficulties and the controversies that surround them. Instead, we want to help you understand some basic facts, and we want you to see how these facts support your faith that your Bible is God's Word.

Introduction to Textual Criticism

The field of scholarship that deals with differences in Bible manuscripts is known as *Textual criticism*. In some ways this name is unfortunate, because it seems to suggest an attitude of disrespect toward the Bible. When we think of criticism, we think of jabs like these: "You're dumb." "Your clothes make you look fat." "What a terrible shot!" When you think about it a bit more,

While in college, Johann Albrect Bengel (1687-1752) encountered unbelievers who taught and wrote that tens of thousands of manuscript differences rendered the New Testament untrustworthy. Bengel decided he would study the preservation of the Greek text for himself before accepting these views. Contrary to what he was being taught, he concluded that the variations are remarkably few. He also discovered that no point of doctrine rests on an uncertain text. Bengel's work solidified his belief in verbal inspiration, and he went on to become a leading scholar in the field of textual criticism.

though, you realize that not all criticism is negative. Ten minutes before your date arrives, you may appreciate your mom's or dad's criticism concerning your appearance. And certainly we all like positive critical judgment: "I really like that dress." "You played a great game."

Whether positive or negative, criticism is basically the act of comparing one thing to another and making a decision or an evaluation. The people who give you compliments have judged your clothing or skills in comparison with others and have made a positive evaluation. A television critic judges programs by certain standards, compares them to other programs, and then forms an opinion, favorable or not. So criticism is simply an informed evaluation, a judgment passed by someone who is qualified to render it.

> *The textual critic seeks to determine what most likely was the original wording of the text by comparing the readings that differ.*

But who is qualified to pass judgment on the Bible? Of course, nobody is qualified to decide that something written in the Bible is false. But textual criticism does not deal with questions of truth or error in the Bible. There is another field of biblical criticism that does deal with those questions, and those critics *are* at fault for presuming to pass judgment on the Scripture. But textual criticism restricts itself to questions about what an author actually wrote. Where the manuscripts differ from one another, the textual critic compares the various readings (usually involving no more than a word or a brief phrase), formulates an educated opinion about which one is most likely the original, and makes a decision, which, by the way, is binding on absolutely no one.

Let's conclude our introduction to the field of textual criticism with two important observations. First, you should be aware that the science of textual criticism is not restricted to biblical studies. Serious study of any kind of literature involves questions about what a writer originally wrote in passages where various editions of his work contain different readings. Of course, textual criticism is especially important in the study of hand-copied literature, where such differences are especially numerous. Second, you should understand that textual criticism did not arise as a means of creating doubts about the Bible. Instead, it represents the natural response of people to the discovery that various copies of an important piece of literature contain differences in wording.

Sincere Christians have taken several approaches to some issues related to Bible manuscripts, and they have often entered into controversy over their positions. Without taking up these controversies, we can be thankful that so many scholars have spent so much time studying the differences between these manuscripts. The information they have collected and organized can help build our confidence in the trustworthiness of the Bible we use every day. A little later we will discuss some of this information. First, though, it will be helpful for you to learn more about the materials and methods for making books in ancient times. After all, neither Moses nor Paul could go out and buy a box of stationery or a ream of typing paper when he got ready to write something!

Ancient Books and Writing

No doubt your reaction to the words "Okay, class, take out a half sheet of paper" is something less than ecstatic. But paper itself really is a blessing. How would you like to carry a stack of heavy clay tablets to school every day? Teachers would have trouble, too, lugging home a briefcase full of homework to grade. To be fair, we must admit that clay would have its benefits: clay airplanes would fly farther and faster, and landings would be more

A New Testament parchment manuscript from the fourth century A.D.

A New Testament papyrus manuscript from the third century A.D.

spectacular. Seriously, though, in ancient times people often wrote on clay tablets and pieces of pottery. Such materials obviously put a rather strict limit on how long a piece of writing could be.

The most common material for literary writing in the ancient world was papyrus (from which we get our word *paper*). In fact, probably all the books of the Bible were written on papyrus. Papyrus is a reed found mainly along the Nile River in Egypt, growing as tall as twelve to fifteen feet. The manufacture of writing material involved cutting the reeds into sections about a foot long and slicing the pith (soft interior fibers) into thin strips. Two layers of moist strips, laid at right angles to one another, would be pressed together. After drying and smoothing, a sheet of papyrus became a very good writing surface. For long documents, sheets of papyrus would be glued together end to end and rolled up into a scroll.

The biggest problem with papyrus was that it would rot when exposed to moisture. For this reason it is safe to assume that the original of each book perished shortly after it was written. A more durable writing surface, called parchment, was made of animal skins. The story is told of Eumenes II, king of Pergamum (in Asia Minor), who decided about 190 B.C. that he wanted a library to rival the one in Alexandria, Egypt. He hired the Alexandrian librarian to come to Pergamum to develop his library. Naturally, the pharaoh did not appreciate the competition and threw the librarian into jail. Also, he refused to sell papyrus to the king of Pergamum. Eumenes frantically sought an alternative. When he developed a high quality parchment, he began to promote it as an improvement over papyrus. Because it was durable and readily available, this new, improved parchment replaced papyrus for serious writing—though not until the fourth century A.D.

We mentioned earlier that ancient "books" were actually scrolls of papyrus or parchment, averaging twenty-five or thirty feet in length. Compared to today's books, the scroll format suffered from several serious drawbacks. The fact that one side remained blank represented a waste of writing material. Scrolls were bulky (the Old

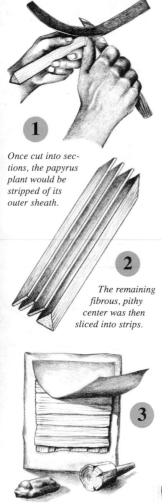

1

Once cut into sections, the papyrus plant would be stripped of its outer sheath.

2

The remaining fibrous, pithy center was then sliced into strips.

3

The strips were then arranged in two layers at right angles to each other. After being hammered together, the layers would form a temporarily durable writing surface.

4

Papyrus sheets were commonly glued together in a scroll format until the second century.

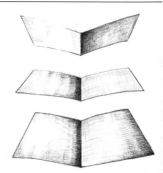

Early in the second century, Christians bega folding and gluing the sheets in a codex form

The side of a papyrus sheet with the grain running horizontally was easier to write on than the side with the grain running vertically. People would use the back side of a sheet only when necessary. This fact helps us understand the significance of the book of God's judgment that John saw, described in Revelation 5:1. This book, says John, was written "within and on the backside." This description suggests that these judgments are so extensive that one side of a scroll cannot contain them; the Lord had to continue writing on the back.

Testament filled fifteen to twenty scrolls—how many points do you suppose bringing your Bible to Sunday school was worth?), and they were cumbersome to use. Imagine a teacher saying to the class, "Open your scrolls to column fifty-three." You would have to unroll with one hand while rolling up with the other, never forgetting to count the columns as you went. Be thankful for the book format we enjoy today!

Let's move on now from the subject of book materials to that of writing itself. For much of the nineteenth and twentieth centuries, liberals have scoffed at the idea that Moses himself wrote the first five books of the Bible. They argue that Moses died long before writing existed in the ancient Near East. They also explain that what Moses taught was passed on orally from generation to generation until someone finally wrote it down.

We know now, however, that writing was widespread hundreds of years before Moses was born. Moses was writing in the late fifteenth century B.C. Archeologists have discovered the written law codes of Hammurabi, an ancient Babylonian king, dating three hundred years before Moses' birth. They have also discovered that slaves were writing on the walls of the salt mines in Egypt at the time of Moses. If slaves could write, certainly Prince Moses could. After all, Acts 7:22 mentions that "Moses was learned in all the wisdom of the Egyptians." Far from being illiterate, Moses probably knew three or four languages!

Manuscripts of the Bible

We come now to the question of how we know that, in spite of their differences, the ancient manuscripts preserve the Word of God. One way to answer this question would be to suggest that one of the manuscripts should serve as the standard against which the others could be corrected. But we could make such a claim only if God guided us to select the right manuscript. In *any* question of truth, the only infallible guide is God Himself. God *has* given us clear leading on many subjects; we find His leading in the Bible. We learn there, for example, that Jesus is the Son of God, who lived a sinless life and died to pay the penalty for man's sin. There can be no question about this truth or about many others clearly taught in the Bible.

But does the Bible tell us which of its manuscripts contains the inspired text down to the smallest detail? Thankfully, it does not. We must search for our answer along other lines.

Are you surprised that we think this silence is a blessing? Think about this for a moment. Though such insight would simplify matters considerably, it would come at an awful price. We would have to conclude that God inspired an errant text, for no existing manuscript is perfect in every detail. But suppose God preserved a *perfect* manuscript that exactly preserved His Word.

> *The imperfections in the manuscripts are so minor that they have absolutely no bearing on the overall doctrines of Scripture.*

Wouldn't that be a blessing? No. Such a manuscript would present a strong temptation to idolatry. People in false religions often worship items such as bones, stones, and bits of cloth thought to have been associated with some godly saint or with the Lord Jesus Himself. People do this because human nature tends to venerate objects instead of worshiping God in spirit (John 4:20-24). A manuscript that was the Word of God in all its perfection would certainly become an object of worship, detracting from the glory of its author.

So we cannot claim that there is a single manuscript containing every single word, just as God inspired it. Instead, God has caused His Truth to spread throughout the world in copies that He has allowed to contain slight imperfections. The imperfections are so minor that they have absolutely no bearing on the doctrines of

- *Preservation:* God's work causing His Word to remain available in every generation
- *Textual Criticism:* the science of evaluating different manuscripts and forming opinions about which reading is most likely to be the original
- *Reading:* a specific form of a certain passage in a manuscript, usually restricted to a single word or a brief phrase.
- *Manuscript:* an ancient handwritten copy of some portion of Scripture

Scripture. There are no manuscripts that fail to present the essential truth about God's holiness, man's sin, and the gracious redemption provided in Christ.

These imperfections have never been an obstacle to faith for people who are inclined to believe. In fact, though God has not told us this in just so many words, it seems that He has purposely provided ammunition that people who hate Him can use to attack Him and to justify their refusal to believe. These minor difficulties, then, serve as a test of true faith that helps to separate the "sheep" from the "goats" (Matt. 25:32).

Looking Ahead to Part 2

It may seem uncomfortable for this lesson to end on a somewhat negative note. Remember, though, that this lesson is only Part 1 of the subject before us. In Part 2 we will help you recognize that lacking a perfect copy of God's Word need not rob us of our confidence in Scripture. God has preserved a great wealth of evidence supporting the conclusion that we do have God's Word today.

Review Questions

1. What two basic human activities has God used to preserve His Word in our language?

    manuscript copying and translation

2. Our word *paper* comes from the name of what ancient writing material? *papyrus*

3. The development of what writing material resulted from political and economic conflict between two nations?

4. The law codes of Hammurabi prove what important point about the Bible's reliability?

5. What is wrong with the following statement? "At the time of Christ, the biggest problem with books was their tendency to fall apart at the spine."

_____6. Differences among Bible manuscripts have been cited by unbelievers as proof that the wording of modern Bibles is unreliable.

_____7. Our understanding of the Bible's preservation rests solely on the facts of history.

_____8. There is no such thing as constructive criticism; criticism by its very nature is destructive.

Multiple Choice

_____9. Which of the following is not true?

A. Only a few of the original manuscripts written by the Scripture writers themselves have survived until today.

B. The handwritten copies of the Bible that have come down to us from ancient times contain differences in wording.

C. Every single word that the Scripture writers themselves put on paper was exactly what God wanted, without error.

D. Copies of Scripture written on parchment were much more durable than those written on papyrus.

_____10. In the ancient world, hand copying someone else's work for publication was

A. tolerated as a necessary evil.

B. punishable by imprisonment or death.

C. legal only if the copyist was a professional scribe.

D. a highly valued service.

_____ 11. Textual criticism is the field of scholarship that

    A. attempts to determine the original wording of passages where various copies or editions of a work differ from one another.

    B. examines the factual content of a piece of literature in order to determine its trustworthiness.

    C. attempts to determine whether an author is consistent with himself by comparing the ideas found in his various writings.

    D. compares the works of various authors in order to determine which authors are most reliable.

_____ 12. Textual criticism

    A. is a relatively simple and straightforward field of study.

    B. should be rejected by all who believe the Bible.

    C. has yielded results that increase our confidence that God has preserved His Word.

    D. has determined which ancient manuscripts of the Bible contain no errors.

    E. is a field of study that relates exclusively to the Bible.

_____ 13. Minor imperfections in Bible manuscripts

    A. make it difficult, but not impossible, to trust the Bible.

    B. do not change the character of the Scripture as the Word of God.

    C. have come about despite God's best efforts to prevent them.

    D. make it impossible to determine the message of the Bible.

14. Explain why J. A. Bengel became interested in textual criticism and how this study affected his thinking about the New Testament.

15. When unbelievers compare manuscripts, they find differences that they take as justification for their unbelief. When believers compare manuscripts, they find a degree of similarity that strengthens their faith. Explain how these two groups can look at the same evidence and come to opposite conclusions.

16. Explain why the term *textual criticism* does not imply an unbelieving attitude toward the Bible.

17. Suggest two possible reasons for the Bible's not telling us which manuscripts preserve God's Word.

Do You Have God's Word Today? *Part 2*

(4)

Heb 12-29 , John 4:24

Where We've Been and Where We're Going

In Part 1 of our discussion you explored some historical background about the hand copying of Bible manuscripts and learned something about the science of textual criticism. All this has focused on the issue of the preservation of God's Word in its original languages. In this lesson we will finish that aspect of the question of how we can know that we have God's Word today, and we will also go on to examine the second aspect of the question, which is how we can be sure that our translations preserve God's Word in our own language.

The Accuracy of Old Testament Manuscripts

Because of its age, the Old Testament has been especially criticized as inaccurate. The existing manuscripts are copies of copies of copies of copies, and each new copy not only perpetuated earlier copying errors but also added new errors of its own.

GET THE BIG PICTURE

❑ Historical background
❑ The preservation of Scripture in the original languages: the science of textual criticism
  • Goal pursued by textual criticism
  • Materials available for textual criticism
  • Conclusion drawn by textual criticism: God has preserved His Word
    - Preservation of the Old Testament
    - Preservation of the New Testament
❑ The preservation of Scripture in translations

Note: The shaded portions appear in Part 1.

You can correct some copying errors by comparing newer copies with older ones, but the oldest Old Testament manuscripts that we have were produced up to thirteen hundred years after the original writings. Until recently, the oldest Hebrew manuscript we had was from the tenth century A.D., nearly twenty-three hundred years after the time of Moses. Bible-believing Christians' only response to these charges was simply to trust that God had accurately preserved His Word. Today two factors combine to bolster our confidence in the trustworthiness of the Old Testament text.

The Method of the Scribes

The first factor is the care with which the scribes copied the Old Testament. Jewish tradition relates that after Ezra the scribe finished II Chronicles and compiled the canonical books, he formed a school of scribes to be the guardians of the text. As time passed, the scribes developed an elaborate system of tests to insure the accuracy of their work. For example, they noted in the margin any word that occured only once in the Bible. If the word appeared elsewhere in a later copy, then the scribe knew there had been a mistake. The scribes also kept track of the number of letters and words in each book. For each book they knew the middle word and letter, and they even knew how many times each letter occurred. After finishing a book, they would check their work. If it did not pass and they could not find the problem, they would destroy the copy and begin again. Talk about frustration! Imagine having to recopy Isaiah!

Later Jews also had a high view of Scripture. Knowing that there was a curse on any who would add to or take away from the Word of God, they were extremely careful not to alter the text in any way. Only a trained scribe was allowed to copy the sacred books. Thus the copying was left to an elite group with great skills, great care in checking their work, and an exalted view of the Word of God.

Christ Himself testified to these scribes' successful preservation of the Old Testament Scriptures. The Lord often quoted from the Old Testament, but He never designated a particular manuscript or group of manuscripts as corrupt or doctrinally incorrect. Had there been any cause for doubt, He certainly would have specified which text had the authority of Scripture. Thus, we are confident there was no significant change in the text during those four thousand years.

However, the Old Testament text had to pass through another fifteen centuries of hand copying before the age of movable type printing in Europe. How do we know it survived unchanged during that period? Critics often charged that the rate of change would have been so great that after a few centuries the text would have been unidentifiable with its prototype. After all, the oldest available manuscript went back to only the tenth century. Though that was one thousand years ago, it was still one thousand years *since* the time of Christ. But a startling discovery made just after World War II finally put this question to rest.

The Discovery of the Dead Sea Scrolls

In November or December of 1946, three Bedouin shepherds were tending their sheep in the Jordan Valley near the Dead Sea. One of the Bedouins had the habit of exploring caves, hoping to find treasure. As he walked along

The caves at Qumran

the base of a cliff, he threw a rock into a cave. To his amazement, he heard some pottery shatter. The shepherd called his two cousins over and described what had just happened. Because it was so late, they agreed to explore the cave together later. Being

One of the Dead Sea Scrolls

too busy the next day, they delayed the exploration further.

Early on the third day the youngest cousin, Muhammed the Wolf, arose before dawn and slipped away to the cave alone. He slid in through a small opening and found several large earthen jars and some broken pottery. Only one jar contained anything of interest—three leather scrolls. Muhammed pulled out the scrolls and returned to camp. When his older cousins found out that he had sneaked off without them to explore the cave, they became angry and would not allow him to have anything more to do with the "treasure." The following March the two older cousins traveled to Bethlehem, where they eventually sold Mohammed's scrolls for $68.47. Later these three scrolls and one other were sold for $250,000 to the nation of Israel and are now displayed in the Shrine of the Book Museum in Jerusalem.

Since then tens of thousands of fragments from hundreds of manuscripts have been discovered in various caves around the Dead Sea. Part or all of every book of the Old Testament except Esther has been found. Many other documents have also been found, including books from the Apocrypha. All these finds date back to between 200 B.C. and A.D. 100.

The Shrine of the Book Museum, which houses some of the Dead Sea Scrolls

One of the most impressive manuscripts is the Isaiah scroll, one of Muhammed's original three. It is a leather scroll in good condition, containing almost the entire prophecy. This scroll dates back to 100 B.C., about a thousand years earlier than any Hebrew manuscript previously known. Here was the real test. How closely would the modern text match this old manuscript? *The texts were almost identical.* In fact, a committee using the scroll to translate Isaiah for a new English version found only thirteen points at which they preferred the scroll's wording over that of the traditional text.

These manuscript finds near the Dead Sea are among the most significant archeological discoveries of the century, and perhaps of all time. They forever shattered the view of liberal scholars that the original text of the Old Testament was hopelessly lost through centuries of copying. Now we possess physical evidence demonstrating that the Hebrew text used in Jesus' day agrees with the text we currently use.

The Accuracy of New Testament Manuscripts

The manuscript evidence for the New Testament has an entirely different complexion. In some respects it is even stronger than the evidence for the Old Testament, while in other respects it is not. Like the Old Testament evidence, it gives us strong assurance that God has preserved His Word.

Number and Age of the Manuscripts

The evidence for the text of the New Testament is far superior to that of the Old in terms of nearness to the time of writing. Among the more than five thousand Greek manuscripts (not to mention thousands of copies of early translations into other languages), more than a few date to within two hundred years of the original. The oldest known manuscript, containing a small portion of John 18, was copied perhaps as soon as twenty-five years after John died.

The oldest New Testament manuscript, containing a portion of John 18 (A.D. 125)

That we have so many manuscripts of the New Testament from so early a period sets it apart from all other books as unique. For example, Homer's *Iliad*, the most popular book of the Greek speaking world, exists in only 647 manuscripts. Aristotle wrote around 340 B.C., and we have only five Greek manuscripts of any of his works, the earliest dating around A.D. 1100. Some lengthy passages from ancient authors have come down to us in only a single manuscript. Yet no one seriously questions whether we have the words of these authors. Why, then, should we question whether we have the Word of God? The manuscripts are so abundant that the New Testament scholar who compares his field to that of any other ancient literature feels almost guilty about the wealth of evidence available to him.

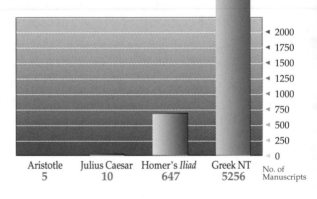

Aristotle	Julius Caesar	Homer's *Iliad*	Greek NT	No. of Manuscripts
5	10	647	5256	

Care in Copying the Manuscripts

Although New Testament manuscripts approach more closely the time of writing than do those of the Old, they contain more differences in wording. For several reasons the New Testament copyists were not as careful as the Jewish scribes. First, the copying was not restricted to a certain class of people and, as a result, was not regulated. There was no systematic testing for accuracy.

Copyists used various handwriting styles and abbreviations. While many copyists were painstakingly careful, a few were very sloppy and careless. Most, of course, simply did the best they could within practical limits.

A second reason for inaccuracy was the haste with which many books were copied. When Paul wrote a letter to a church, other churches in the area wanted copies as soon as possible. As Christianity spread, the demand for copies exceeded the supply. Wealthy patrons would spend great amounts of money for personal copies. The faster one could copy, the richer one became.

Yet another reason for mistakes in some copies arose from a method of copying that was developed to increase efficiency. In this method, one person would read a manuscript to a room full of copyists who wrote what they heard. To minimize errors, a corrector would check the work afterward. Still, some copying errors escaped notice.

You should not get the idea, though, that New Testament manuscripts are hopelessly at odds with one another. Repeatedly textual critics have observed that in over ninety-five percent of the text, these manuscripts agree with each other in the smallest details. Furthermore, no manuscript differs from another in the essential teachings of the New Testament. When we consider that the copying took place throughout Europe, North Africa, and

Western Asia over a period of some fourteen hundred years, the remarkable thing is not that these five thousand manuscripts differ from one another but that they are so strikingly alike.

Summary of Manuscript Evidence

God did not choose to do a miracle and preserve a perfect text of Scripture. When you think about it, though, the preservation of God's Word in the mass of manuscripts is for all practical purposes miraculous. Centuries of painstaking textual criticism have yielded results that give us absolute assurance regarding more than ninety-five percent of the individual words of the New Testament; the percentage for the Old is even higher. Most of the five percent in question are matters of word order and other differences that have little or no effect on the meaning. Even the few passages in which the meaning is questionable do not leave us in any doubt about any doctrine of Scripture. The doctrines in those passages in question are clearly taught in other passages in which the manuscripts agree. The textual evidence for the New Testament is so strong that if you constructed a Bible from the very worst manuscripts (those that differ most extensively from all the others), you would still have overwhelming testimony to the character of God and the way of salvation.

Think about how God works. Sometimes He does something that defies the laws of nature. Miracles of this type include Israel's crossing the Red Sea, Jesus' turning the water into wine, and so on. At other times, though, God simply engineers natural processes to achieve His goals. The story of Esther seems

A portion of the Leningrad Codex (A.D. 1000) showing Genesis 1:25-26

designed to emphasize this fact. None of that book's events appears to be miraculous. Yet the way the circumstances work together to secure the deliverance of God's people makes it clear that God Himself was at work. In the same way, God seems to have used "natural" circumstances and processes to preserve such a wealth of textual evidence supporting our Bible that, in hindsight, we realize that something supernatural has taken place.

Translations

What we have discussed so far relates to the preservation of God's Word in its original languages. Very few teenagers, however, have ever seen a copy of the Scripture in its original languages. We hope you have found our discussion of the ancient manuscripts profitable, but we realize that you are probably more concerned about the trustworthiness of your English Bible than about that of the manuscripts. Can you say with confidence that the Bible you hold in your hands is the Word of God?

Lost in Translation?

The issue, you recall, is whether God has preserved the words of Scripture. Of course, by its very nature, translation involves changing words. Sometimes the change is simple; the translator merely substitutes for a word in one language a simple equivalent in the other. If we could translate every word of Scripture this way, there would be no question about whether the resulting translation is truly the Word of God. But if you are taking a foreign language course, you know that you often cannot translate

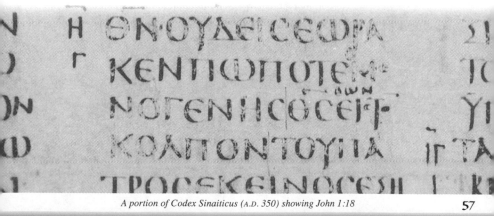

A portion of Codex Sinaiticus (A.D. 350) showing John 1:18

word-for-word without losing the meaning. For example, the English comment on the weather "It's cold" does not transfer word-for-word into Spanish. The Spanish expression for that idea, translated literally into English, is "Makes cold." For a biblical example, consider Matthew 1:18, which says that Jesus was conceived "before they [Mary and Joseph] came together." A strictly literal translation of this phrase would read "before than to come together them." You would quickly become frustrated with Bible reading if your Bible contained such confusing language every few verses!

A translator, then, cannot avoid changing some words, based on his understanding of what the text says and how the languages work. Since human understanding and decisions are imperfect, the only way for a translation to avoid all imperfection would be for God to control the translator just as He controlled the original writer.

Some Christians believe this is exactly what God did in 1611 when the King James Version was translated. If this is so, then our question is answered, for the translation itself is just as inspired as the original writings. While this position seems to simplify the issue of preservation, in the end it produces greater problems. For example, on what basis can we claim that these translators were inspired and others were not? Such a claim is complicated by the fact that the King James translators themselves did not believe they were inspired. Indeed, they recognized their own fallibility. Furthermore, if these men were inspired in the same sense the biblical authors were, how can we account for the fact that sometimes the meaning communicated by the KJV is different from that of the original languages? Should we correct the Greek and Hebrew manuscripts by the KJV? Admittedly, such a difference does not occur on every page, but it need occur only once to make this position quite problematic.

If all translations are subject to human error, can we still say that we have God's Word in our own language? Before we look at some pertinent Scripture portions, let's think about our own experience with translation. Have you ever watched the evening news and observed a newsman interview someone through an interpreter? Did it seem that they could understand each other?

Though the situation may have been somewhat awkward, each person was probably able to express his thoughts to the other quite well. While visiting Israel, I spent an evening with some Christians living in Bethlehem. Just before we left, one man, who didn't know English, prayed for all of us in Arabic. As I was leaving, I asked my host what the man prayed, and with apparent ease he listed several of the requests. It never occurred to me to question whether those ideas were in fact mentioned in the prayer. Why? I assumed—as we all do—that successful translation is not only possible, but that it is also a normal activity among those that know two languages well.

Now consider the New Testament and its world. In the first century A.D., the dominant translation of the Old Testament was the Septuagint. This translation was made around 150 B.C. from Hebrew into Greek, and it was far from ideal by today's standards. Some portions offer a good rendering of the Hebrew. Others, however, are very interpretive and not at all literal. Still other portions are so literal that the sense cannot be understood without comparing the Greek to the original Hebrew. Yet this was the Bible of the early church. In fact, Christ and His apostles frequently quoted from it and never criticized it. In one place the apostle Paul exhorts his Greek-speaking readers to "let the word of Christ dwell in you richly" (Col. 3:16). Since the only Bible these believers could read was the Septuagint, the apostle must have been encouraging Christians to read the Septuagint as "the word of Christ."

But what about the Septuagint? Are Christ and the apostles denying that these problems existed? No, their recommendation of this translation simply demonstrates what Christians throughout history have maintained—that minor mistakes in translation do not harm the character of God's Word. The Word of God is a message and a body of truth that so thoroughly saturates the stories, poetry, preaching, and personal correspondence of Scripture that it simply cannot be destroyed by any faithful attempt to copy or translate it. If the Word of God were so fragile that the slightest human touch could ruin it, we would be in big trouble, and God would be no remarkable author. The miracle and wonder of the Scripture is that God has given it to us in an indestructible form.

Do you own a Bible? Read it! It is God's Word to you. Obey it! Do not be troubled if a preacher or teacher suggests occasionally that a word or two might be understood differently, as long as the suggestion fits well with the Bible's overall teaching. Be thankful for that insight, and don't let it rob you of your confidence that you can trust the Bible you hold in your hands.

Which Translation?

But which Bible should you hold in your hands? You are probably aware of several English translations; perhaps you have wondered what the differences are and which one you should use. The King James Version has long been the standard translation for English-speaking Christians, but newer translations are easier to understand. Is there anything wrong with using a newer translation? This is a controversial question, and you will do well to respect the views of your spiritual leaders. In addition to their advice, here is some general information that can help you on this issue.

Always remember that the original writers of the Bible did not write in English. Nor did they write in Spanish, German, or French. Their language was Hebrew, Aramaic, or Greek. You should be sure that the translation you use reflects accurately the wording of the original languages. Of course, unless you learn these languages yourself, you will be dependent upon someone else's assessment of that accuracy. Learn as much as you can and learn whom to trust.

Also remember that "new" does not automatically mean "liberal." Still, many new translations do push a certain agenda or deny a specific doctrine. Because they do not accurately preserve the meaning of the original texts, they are to be rejected. Beware of a new translation unless you have good reason to trust it.

On the other hand, the "old" translations (of which the King James Version is by far the most important) spring from orthodox theology and are therefore reliable. Their biggest problem is that they are hard to understand. But who said reading the Bible should be easy? We certainly do not want to confine people to a Bible they cannot understand, but the study of Scripture will always require discipline and diligent effort. A translation that takes the work out of Bible study is doing too much work for you and robbing you of the benefit. Furthermore, it probably does some of that work incorrectly and robs you of the most accurate meaning.

In closing, let us reiterate what we said above. If you have confidence that the Bible you hold in your hand accurately preserves the meaning of the Greek and Hebrew, there is no reason to wonder whether you have the Word of God. Thank God for it. Read it. Trust it. Obey it.

Conclusion

We have now covered the theological and historical portion of the question "How do I know the Bible is true?" Paul's declaration that "All scripture is given by inspiration of God" (II Tim. 3:16) means that the Holy Spirit supernaturally guided the writers of the sixty-six canonical books so that the words they wrote were the very words God intended. Furthermore, we can have confidence that God has preserved the wording of these books for us today.

At this point you may be saying, "You've been using the Bible to prove itself. Isn't this circular reasoning?" Up to this point, the material presented is specifically for you, the Christian teenager. But what if you were defending the Bible to someone who didn't believe its claims in the first place? Would they accept these verses? Probably not. In the next lesson we will look at some evidences outside the Bible that support its claims to be the Word of God.

Review Questions

1. According to tradition, what Old Testament character gave very careful attention to the preservation of the exact wording of the Hebrew text?

2. In order for a translation to be perfect in every word, God must have

____3. The accuracy of Old Testament manuscripts has never been seriously questioned, because some of the existing manuscripts were copied within a few years of the original writing.

____4. Which of the following statements about Bible manuscripts is true?

   A. False religions have arisen based on a few manuscripts that are full of doctrinal errors.
   B. Each manuscript presents the same essential truths and doctrines.
   C. The oldest manuscripts in existence are no nearer to the time of writing than five hundred years.
   D. A few existing manuscripts contain the original text precisely as God inspired it.

_____5. Which of the following statements about Bible transla-
tions is false?

    A. It is impossible to translate from one language to an-
other without changing words.

    B. Textual critics concentrate their study on evaluating
the accuracy of the translations.

    C. Some Bible translations are untrustworthy and
should be rejected.

    D. The most important point on which to evaluate a
Bible translation is the accuracy with which it reflects the wording of the original languages.

_____6. The Dead Sea Scrolls

    A. are the only manuscripts ever discovered that are ac-
tually older than the original writings.

    B. have revolutionized the textual criticism of the New
Testament.

    C. guided the translators of the King James Version in
resolving textual questions.

    D. have confirmed the trustworthiness of the traditional
text of the Hebrew Old Testament.

_____7. The Isaiah Scroll

    A. finally revealed the true text of many obscure pas-
sages in the book.

    B. is nearly identical in wording to manuscripts copied
one thousand years later.

    C. was destroyed by vandals before scholars studied it.

    D. is written in Isaiah's own handwriting.

_____8. If a New Testament were put together from the manu-
scripts copied most poorly, it would

    A. differ very little from the New Testament as you
know it.

    B. be full of dangerous errors found in heretical manu-
scripts.

    C. obscure the character of God and the way of salvation.

    D. be easier to understand than the New Testament as
you know it.

_____9. A translation so easy to read that it takes the work out of Bible study would be

    A. welcomed by all Christians.

    B. doing too much work for the reader.

    C. easy to create if Christians would stop arguing about translation philosophy.

    D. impossible to create without the insights of modern textual criticism.

_____10. What should be your attitude toward the Bible translation you are expected to use?

    A. Read, believe, and obey it.

    B. Be suspicious of its teaching since no translation is perfect.

    C. Never consider the possibility that even a single word of it could be improved.

    D. Be ready to replace it with a newer version since newer versions are better than older ones.

_____11. Which of the following statements compares most accurately the strength of manuscript evidence for the Old Testament and that for the New?

    A. The New Testament evidence is stronger in terms of the number of manuscripts and their age but not as strong in terms of the manuscripts' similarity to one another.

    B. The New Testament evidence is stronger in every way.

    C. The legibility of Old Testament manuscripts makes up for what they lack in attention to detail.

    D. There is no significant difference between them.

_____12. Which of the following attitudes toward new translations is most dangerous?

    A. Reject them without questioning.

    B. Accept them without questioning.

    C. Accept them if they prove accurate to the original Greek and Hebrew.

    D. Reject them if they are viewed by some Christians as defective.

_____13. The past two lessons devote more space to the subject of the preservation of God's Word in the original languages than to the subject of Bible translations. Which of the following statements seems to give the best reason for this emphasis?

    A. Since the original languages are the more obscure subject, they are more suitable for academic study.

    B. The original languages are the more controversial subject, requiring more detailed discussion.

    C. The preservation of the original languages is the fundamental issue, since a translation can be no more accurate than the original-language manuscripts.

    D. The original languages are the more commonly discussed subject, requiring you to be more prepared to defend your position.

Essay

14. Contrast the manuscript evidence for Aristotle's writings with the manuscript evidence for the New Testament.

15. Discuss several reasons that the New Testament manuscripts differ from one another more than those of the Old.

16. Is the preservation of Scripture miraculous or not? Explain.

More Evidence? Read On!

(5)

Memory Verses: Matthew 16:16-17

Keeping Evidence in Its Proper Place

Let's start this lesson by summarizing what we have covered so far. Everyone wants reliable information, especially regarding life-and-death issues. We have claimed that the Bible is reliable because it comes from the ultimate reliable source. When it comes to life and death, God is the expert because He created all, sees all, and controls all. He is infallible, and so is His book. But the question "How do you *really* know?" keeps nagging us. We have used the Bible to prove itself, but if the Bible is not entirely reliable, we cannot trust its claim to be God's Word. How can you know that the Bible is true?

"Proving" the trustwortiness of the Bible should be no different than proving any book's reliability: we collect evidence, weigh that evidence, and then draw reasonable conclusions—or is it different? We must remember that if the Bible is God's Word, it is the supreme authority by which all evidence and arguments must be judged. Furthermore, if the Bible's explanation of man's spiritual condition is correct, human beings cannot accurately evaluate the proof for the Bible's reliability. Men are sinners, unwilling to face the truth about themselves and the holy God that made them. Evidence alone—no matter how compelling—cannot convince fallen humans to believe the Bible.

❏ Evidence from Science
  • Biology
  • Medicine
  • Earth Science
❏ Evidence from Archeology
  • Geography
  • History

❏ Evidence from Prophecy
  • Daniel
  • Isaiah
❏ Evidence from Personal Testimony
  • A Chicago Gangster
  • Down-and-Outers
  • Those on the Deathbed

Our Lord's earthly ministry demonstrated this truth in a striking way. Two groups of people observed Jesus closely for three years: Christ's disciples and the Pharisees. The disciples were common, uneducated fishermen, and the Pharisees were well-trained biblical scholars. Both groups had heard that Jesus of Nazareth was God's Messiah (John 1:41; Matt. 26:63-64), and both saw many miracles designed to prove that claim. They knew that Jesus could heal the crippled, give sight to the blind, and even raise the dead. Each group, however, responded differently to Jesus' ministry. Amazingly, those most familiar with the Scripture rejected Him as a demon-possessed blasphemer and therefore demanded His crucifixion. The uneducated fishermen, on the other hand, died martyrs' deaths because they proclaimed Him as the Son of God. Why did these two groups respond differently?

In His conversation with a Pharisee, Jesus indicated the reason these religious leaders rejected Him. Nicodemus approached Jesus one night and willing acknowledged Him as "a teacher come from God" (John 3:2). But he resisted being born again. Nicodemus claimed that Christ's message was difficult to understand and needed to be clarified and validated: "How can a man be born when he is old?" he inquired (John 3:4). Jesus, however, knew that Nicodemus's quandary was due not to a lack of information or evidence. His problem was sin. Without qualification Christ asserted, "He that believeth not is condemned. . . . And this is the condemnation, that light is come into the world, and men loved darkness rather than light, because their deeds were evil" (John 3:18-19). People reject the gospel not because evidence for belief is inconclusive. They reject the truth because they love the darkness of their sin rather than Jesus Christ, the Light of the world.

Why, then, did the disciples receive Jesus as the Messiah? God changed them. As His earthly ministry neared its close, Jesus asked the disciples who they thought He was. Peter, speaking for the disciples, responded confidently, "Thou art the Christ, the Son of the living God" (Matt. 16:16). Interestingly, Christ did not attribute Peter's correct confession to the miracles he saw, his unusual spiritual insight, or even his willingness to obey God's will. Jesus explained that Peter had grasped His true identity because God had revealed Himself to him: "Blessed art thou, Simon Barjona: for flesh and blood hath not revealed it unto thee, but my Father which is in heaven" (Matt. 16:17).

Think about your conversion. Did you become a Christian because someone proved to you that the Bible is true? Most likely you received the Lord because you were overwhelmed with your own sinfulness. Since the Scripture offered you forgiveness and eternal life, you repented and believed the gospel. It wasn't the "undeniable evidence" that moved you. Through the Holy Spirit, the Father convicted and changed your heart.

Now let's return to our original question: "How do you know the Bible is true?" We know the Bible is true because God has convinced us that it is true. How do we know He has convinced us? *The Scripture captivates our hearts.* Every time the Bible is attacked, our souls leap to its defense. Whenever it is vindicated, we swell with joy and satisfacton. When it speaks comfort, we take comfort. Whenever it calls us to action, we are moved.

Consequently, when witnessing, we must not tell an unbeliever that evidence alone will convince him to trust the Bible. He, like the Pharisees, may carefully consider our "proofs" and still find them unconvincing because he can think of another way to account for the evidence. Before our carefully crafted arguments can be effective, the skeptic must experience the Father's mysterious yet powerful work in his heart. Then the evidence will become as compelling for him as it is for us. Until he knows that change, we must focus on calling him to forsake his sin and believe the gospel, as Christ dealt with Nicodemus.

Nevertheless, both the saved and unsaved can profit from the four kinds of evidence presented in this lesson. The apostles themselves regularly appealed to the fact that they were eyewitnesses of Jesus' miracles (Acts 2:32; I Cor. 15:1-11; II Pet. 1:16).

God frequently uses such proofs when He brings a person to conversion, though it is God that changes the person—not the evidence. This evidence can also help us as believers. Because we have believed, we can effectively evaluate the evidence for believing. "Through faith we understand" because faith is "the evidence of things not seen" (Heb. 11:1, 3). By reviewing the objective bases for our faith, we grow in the confidence that the Bible's teachings are not "cunningly devised fables" (II Pet. 1:16). Thus, we realize anew that embracing Christ is not a leap in the dark but a leap into the light.

Evidence from Science

 Have you ever looked at an old science textbook? Along with pictures of people in funny clothes with weird hairstyles, you will find concepts and theories that are out-of-date. For example, scientists have recently changed their ideas concerning the nature of the atom. The idea of the nucleus surrounded by orbiting electrons is now obsolete. Protons and neutrons, formerly considered the smallest particles of matter, can now be subdivided into quarks. Someday this "knowledge" is likely to give way to further discoveries. Genetics is another area of technological explosion. Scientists can now clone living organisms, something thought impossible a short time ago. Man broadens his horizons when he develops stronger microscopes and telescopes or arrives at a better system for collecting and analyzing data. As communications technology allows information to spread faster and more widely, mankind is continually revising scientific theories to match new discoveries. In such an advanced age, ancient literature seems almost absurd when it comes to science and medicine—ancient literature, that is, other than the Bible. The Bible rises above the thinking of its day both by avoiding errors and by stating facts that the ancient world seems not to have known. Some of its teachings are so advanced that they were not even understood until fairly recently. Here are some examples from various branches of science.

Biology

Leviticus 17:11 states, "For the life of the flesh is in the blood." Moses made this statement about 1445 B.C. Thousands of years later, physicians believed that many diseases should be treated by letting out "bad" blood. But, for some reason, the patients kept dying. Now we know how important blood is for sustaining life. Organizations like the Red Cross hold blood drives regularly in order to have blood available for people who have lost too much. Rather than take blood away, we put blood in. Modern science has been a little slow in "discovering" this truth stated by Moses more than three thousand years ago.

How did Moses know that blood was necessary for life? We cannot know whether God told Moses directly or whether Moses learned this fact from some human source. What we do know is that Moses, under divine inspiration, wrote the truth.

Medicine

The Bible helped Scottish doctor James Simpson to bring about a major advance in medicine. As a surgeon in the nineteenth century, he was troubled over the trauma endured by patients undergoing surgery. Often the pain was so great that the patient died on the operating table. Simpson wanted to find a way for his patients to be unconscious during the ordeal. One day he called some friends together to try out a new gas he had discovered. As they talked, Dr. Simpson uncorked the bottle. Sometime later when the doctor regained consciousness, he noticed that all of his friends had passed out too. Within a week, Dr. Simpson had used this anesthetic, chloroform, in several operations and childbirths.

At first there was strong opposition to the use of chloroform during childbirth. Many argued that God intended for women to

DID YOU KNOW? George Washington was a victim of the practice of bleeding sick patients. On December 12, 1799, he traveled by horseback for several hours through cold and snow. Doctors treated the resulting severe case of laryngitis by bleeding him. After four heavy bleedings, Washington died on December 14.

suffer in childbirth and that chloroform circumvented God's purposes. It was then that James Simpson realized that putting a patient to sleep before surgery was not new. Genesis 2:21 reads, "And the Lord God caused a deep sleep to fall upon Adam, and he slept: and he took one of his ribs, and closed up the flesh instead thereof." Thousands of years before 1847, God had put His patient to sleep before operating on him. This argument was enough to convince Queen Victoria. She gave birth to her seventh child under the influence of this anesthetic. For the English, the matter was settled, and Dr. Simpson was knighted for his discovery.

Earth Science

Job, who lived probably about the time of Abraham, declared that God "hangeth the earth upon nothing" (Job 26:7). How did he know this? Obviously, he did not have access to telescopes, satellites, or space shuttles. The theory commonly accepted by the ancients pictured the earth as a circular plate supported by four elephants standing on a big sea turtle. We know the truth today because we now have the benefit of Galileo's telescope, Johannes Kepler's discoveries regarding the orbit of the earth around the sun, and many observations made from outer space. But how did Job know? God must have told him.

In contrast to other ancient literature, the Bible is strikingly accurate in its statements about various matters of science and medicine. For a book that is thousands of years old, it is remarkably up-to-date. This book can be only God's doing.

Evidence from Archeology

Within the past one hundred years, archeology has unearthed a number of finds that validate the accuracy of God's Word in matters of geography and history. Christian archeologists have rejoiced at these findings, which have forced even their non-Christian colleagues to respect the accuracy of the biblical record.

W. F. Albright

Many scholars consider William Foxwell Albright (1891-1971) the greatest archeologist of his generation—a generation that witnessed an explosion of archeological discoveries relating to the Bible. Though Albright never changed many of his unbelieving positions concerning the Scripture, archeology did force him to reconsider much of the liberalism he had been taught.

"I defend the substantial historicity of patriarchal tradition [the narratives in Genesis]. . . . I have not surrendered a single position with regard to early Israelite monotheism but, on the contrary, consider the Mosaic tradition as even more reliable than I did. . . . I now recognize that Israelite law and religious institutions tend to be older and more continuous than I had supposed—in other words, I have grown more conservative in my attitude to Mosaic tradition."

—*From the Stone Age to Christianity*, (Garden City, New York: Doubleday, 1957), p. 2.

Geography

When the nation of Israel was established in 1948, Jews who were displaced during World War II flooded the tiny country of Palestine. Because the country was practically a desert, there was a dire need for more water sources. To find new water supplies, the state of Israel hired an archeologist named Nelson Glueck, well known for his success in using the Bible to locate ancient sites. Mr. Glueck simply took his Bible in hand and looked for texts describing water sources. He found these locations and instructed his men to dig there. Wherever they dug, they found water.

Glueck made another important contribution to Israel's economy based on Deuteronomy 8:9, which describes Israel as "a land whose stones are iron, and out of whose hills thou mayest dig brass." At the time, Israel was not known for its vast mineral deposits. In fact, many thought Glueck was on a wild goose chase in trying to prove that verse accurate. But Glueck's conviction was strengthened by other verses in I Kings and I Chronicles indicating that copper mining and metal working took place in Israel. After a lengthy search, he discovered the ancient copper mines in the south of Israel dating back to the time of Solomon. These mines had vast mineral resources that were far from exhausted.

History

Archeology has also been helpful in validating the historical accuracy of biblical accounts. At one time, liberals believed that there was no such person as King Belshazzar. Daniel 5 records that Belshazzar, the son of Nebuchadnezzar, was the king of Babylon on the night the city fell to the Persians. On that evening, God had written a message on a palace wall, announcing the inevitable doom of the kingdom. Unable to interpret the writing, Belshazzar summoned Daniel and promised him the third highest position in the kingdom if he could explain what the writing meant. Until recently the Bible's record of a king named Belshazzar was unsupported by any other historical source. Nebuchadnezzar's son, ancient historians tell us, was Evil-Merodach, and the king when Babylon fell was Nabonidus. Obviously, the biblical account did not match historical records.

A recent archeological discovery of an ancient library has cleared up this apparent discrepancy. From it we learn that although Nabonidus was king of Babylon when the city fell, he had been away from the city for some time, down in the southern part of his empire. In his absence, he had appointed his son, Belshazzar, to rule in his stead. This explains why Daniel was awarded the *third* highest position in the kingdom; it was the highest position Belshazzar could give. Furthermore, ancient Egyptian records indicate that "son" did not have to mean the actual son or even a descendant of the king. It could simply refer to kingly succession.

A cuneiform tablet that mentions Belshazzar by name

Apparently, the person who wrote the book of Daniel had a firsthand account of the court life in Babylon, since accounts written in antiquity seem unaware of Belshazzar. These finds strengthen our faith that Daniel himself wrote the book that bears his name.

Another example of archeology's importance in disproving the critics' view that the Bible is a collection of myths and legends was the discovery of Boghazkoy, the capital city of the Hittite Empire. The Bible mentions the Hittites several times and indicates that they were a powerful people. Until the last hundred years or so, however, historians could not find one scrap of evidence (outside the Bible) that this empire existed. The discovery of Boghazkoy confirms that the Hittites were a powerful people located in the region of modern-day Turkey. Once again, the Bible proves to be correct.

So we see that the Bible is uniquely accurate in areas of science and medicine thousands of years prior to modern theories. The accuracy of details concerning geography and history indicates that the writers were writing firsthand accounts at the time the books were reported to have been written.

The evidences we have studied so far demonstrate the Bible's reliability, but most of them do not deal directly with the issue of divine origin. We will now examine two other kinds of evidence that go further in showing that God must be the author of this inerrant book.

Evidence from Prophecy

The first supernatural evidence we will consider deals with the accuracy with which Old Testament prophets foretold future events. We will focus our attention on one prophecy from Daniel and one from Isaiah.

Daniel

Daniel 8 records a vision of a ram and a goat, a vision given to Daniel during the third year of the reign of Belshazzar, king of

Babylon. In verses 20-22, an angel explains to Daniel the meaning of the dream. The ram stands for the Medo-Persian Empire; the goat stands for the kingdom of Greece that arose and destroyed the Persian Empire. The goat sports a single horn that is broken at the peak of its power; this horn represents Alexander the Great. Alexander died at the age of thirty-three, despairing that he had no more worlds to conquer. His kingdom was then divided among four of his generals, just as the prophecy predicted by picturing four horns sprouting in place of the broken one.

Since Daniel lived about two hundred years prior to Alexander the Great, it is obvious that he could not have predicted these political developments on his own. Granted, he might have been able to guess that Babylon would soon fall. He probably could see "the handwriting on the wall" that Persia was gaining power. But in Daniel's time, Greece was nothing but a collection of tiny city-states engaged in constant war with one another. For Daniel to foresee that Greece would become a world power would be like someone today foreseeing that Rwanda, a small nation whose recent history is filled with civil strife, will one day dominate the world. But Daniel did not stop there; he also predicted that Greece would come to power under the leadership of a single individual whose reign would be cut short and whose kingdom would be divided among four successors.

The facts of history leave us with only three possible conclusions: either Daniel was an incredible guesser, someone else wrote the "prophecy" after the fact, or God revealed the information to Daniel. The first option is in fact incredible, in the strict sense of the word ("impossible to believe"). We can also rule out the second possibility because the historical details and the writing style signal that the book was written at the time of Daniel. We are left with the third answer: God must have revealed this prophetic information to Daniel. The Bible is the Word of God.

Isaiah

Isaiah 45:1 reveals in another remarkable prophecy that God had anointed a king named Cyrus to do great things. Isaiah 44:28 reveals that Cyrus would permit Israelite captives to return to their land and rebuild the city of Jerusalem. Isaiah wrote about 150 years before Cyrus was even born. The Jews were still in the land of Palestine; none of them were captives in another land. The Babylonian Empire that would conquer Judah did not yet exist.

How could Isaiah know that all this would happen and even identify the deliverer by name? Could it have been coincidence? It would be as though one might guess that a George Snowcroft will be president of the United States two hundred years from now. We cannot even be positive that the United States will still exist then as we know it today. Can *you* name a person who, in two hundred years, will lead a nation? *God* must have spoken to Isaiah.

The Bible's claims are further strengthened when we consider that no one has ever proved a prophecy to be false. Many skeptics have sought to discredit the Bible and would jump at the chance to exploit a false prophecy, but they cannot do so. All these fulfilled prophecies lead to an obvious conclusion. A human prophet may hit a few guesses, but no man guesses right every single time. Only God can accurately foretell the future.

Cuneiform cylinder seal similar to the one that records Cyrus's release of the Jewish captives

Evidence from Personal Testimony

Since people cannot observe these fulfilled prophecies first-hand, they may excuse such evidence as inconclusive. People demand visible proof that they can see today. This demand leads us to the most powerful external evidence of the Bible's claims as the Word of God—the testimony of changed lives.

A Chicago Gangster

George Mensik was a right-hand man of Chicago gangster Al "Scarface" Capone. From 1925-31, Capone controlled the

George
Mensik

underworld of Chicago crime. As wicked as George Mensik was, God began to work in his heart. Mensik's wife and five-year-old daughter trusted Jesus Christ as Savior and started praying for Mensik's salvation. Burdened with guilt over their pleas, he came home drunk one day, determined to shoot them both. He picked up a loaded pistol and walked into his daughter's room. As he pointed the gun at the kneeling figure of the girl beside her bed, he heard her small voice crying up to God to save her dad. Mensik broke down and shortly thereafter received Christ.

George Mensik's life changed dramatically. His life was in great danger for a few years. Thugs would jump from black limousines and shoot at his house. But even in the midst of the persecution, he had joy and peace in his heart. He had a prison ministry and was able to lead many souls to Christ. The state of Illinois completely cleared his criminal record. Once able to eat ice cream and laugh while his henchmen tortured somebody, as a Christian he would weep over lost souls and the effects of sin in people's lives.

Down-and-Outers

Another story is told of the famous preacher Harry Ironside. He was visiting a street meeting in San Francisco and was asked to preach. While on the platform, Dr. Ironside was handed a card on which a well-known agnostic had written a challenge for a debate the following Sunday afternoon. The topic would be "Agnosticism versus Christianity." After Ironside read the challenge out loud to the crowd, he agreed to the debate on one condition. The agnostic must bring with him one man who had been saved from a life of alcohol and one lady rescued out of a life of prostitution due to their belief in agnosticism.

Harry
Ironside

For his part, Ironside would bring one hundred such converts to Christ from San Francisco alone. With a smirk on his face and a wave of his hand, the agnostic quietly slipped his way out of the cheering crowd. The Bible is powerful, able to transform the most wicked sinner.

Those on the Deathbed

The Bible is also able to provide peace in a person's heart. Have you ever heard of anyone who, on his deathbed, lamented the fact that he had lived his life as a Christian? On the other hand, many atheists have died discontented, realizing that they had rejected the truth. Consider, for example, the French philosopher Voltaire. One of the most celebrated figures of his day, he used his wit and worldly wisdom to ridicule Christianity and the Bible. But as he lay on his deathbed for two months, he turned against his flatterers with rage: "Begone! It is you that have brought me to my present condition. Leave me, I say; begone! What a wretched glory is this which you have produced to me!" After his death, his nurse is reported to have said often, "For all the wealth in Europe I would not see another infidel die."

Voltaire

On the other hand, consider the last words of Joseph Barker, an American infidel who came to Christ and became a preacher of

---

DID YOU KNOW?

Voltaire once said that within a century of his death, the Bible would be studied only as an antiquarian relic. At another time he said, "In twenty years Christianity will be no more. My single hand shall destroy the edifice it took twelve apostles to rear."

If you were God, how would you deal with such a man? Here's what God did. Within fifty years of Voltaire's death, his house and printing press were in the hands of the Geneva Bible Society, playing a key role in the printing and distribution of the very book Voltaire had scorned!

the gospel. A few days before his death, he spoke these words to his son and two friends: "I wish you to witness that . . . I die in the full and firm belief in Jesus Christ. I am sorry for my past errors; but during the last years of my life I have striven to undo the harm I did, by doing all that I was able to do to serve God, by showing the beauty and religion of His Son, Jesus Christ. I wish you to write and witness this, my last confession of faith, that there may be no doubt about it."

Here is a man who started out like Voltaire, but God's grace reached him and changed him, and his deathbed was entirely different from Voltaire's. The value of an investment lies not in its short-term performance but in what it is worth at its end. A human life is an investment, and the final outcome tells a convincing story: lives lived in rebellion against God's Word end in total loss, but those lived in obedience and faith yield an immeasurable return of peace and satisfaction in Christ. What the Bible accomplishes in the life of a believer is perhaps the strongest testimony to its identity as the Word of God.

Test Yourself!

Someone has well said that your life is the only Bible some people will ever read. Those who read the Bible itself will find there a clear picture of a holy and loving God. What about those who read only your life? What portrait of God do your words and deeds paint? How much holiness is evident? How much genuine love?

Conclusion

What you have learned about external evidences supporting the Bible will help you to face Bible critics with greater confidence. No amount of evidence, however, will force somebody to believe the Bible. Satan has blinded the minds of this world to the light of God's Word. God's gift of faith is necessary for one truly to accept the Bible as God's Word. Certainly our faith is not a leap in the dark since there is much evidence to support it, but faith is necessary nonetheless. If you must defend what you believe to somebody who is searching, pray hard that the Holy Spirit will guide that person to the truth.

If you say that you really believe the Bible is God's Word, then you are acknowledging its power to change lives. Can you list changes in your own life that have come about because of the influence of God's Word? Can you name a bad habit that the Holy Spirit has helped you break through the commands and encouragement of the Scripture? Can you name a good habit that God has helped you to establish in obedience to His Word? Do you sincerely desire that your day-to-day conduct will measure up to God's standards for His own glory and for the good of yourself, your family, and your friends?

This study cannot end as a mere academic exercise. If you accept what we have written as true, you cannot avoid making a decision. The Book that we have argued is true and infallible demands your submission to God. The next move is yours, and what you decide will either confirm or change the course of your life, a course that is headed for one of only two possible outcomes. Which will it be for you?

Review Questions

1. What ancient empire was totally unknown outside biblical records until the nineteenth century?

2. What famous historical figure was pictured in Daniel's vision as a single goat's horn?

3. What Persian king does Isaiah name, 150 years before the king's birth, who would restore captive Jews to their homeland?

4. How many of the Bible's prophecies have ever been proved false?

5. What medical practice commonly accepted two hundred years ago ignores a specific Bible teaching?

6. Name two valuable resources that archeologist Nelson Glueck was able to locate in Palestine based on biblical records.

_____7. Evidence alone cannot convince a person that the Bible is true.

_____8. The reason Belshazzar could not offer Daniel the second position in the kingdom is that Persian law did not allow foreigners to have such high authority.

_____9. Most of the specific charges of inaccuracy brought against the Bible one or two hundred years ago are still being brought against it today.

Multiple Choice

_____10. Using the Bible to prove itself is an example of

    A. circular reasoning.
    B. misguided reasoning.
    C. rectangular reasoning.
    D. historical reasoning.

_____11. Peter became convinced that Jesus of Nazareth was the Son of God because

    A. he heard Jesus teach day after day.
    B. he saw Jesus' many miracles.
    C. God the Father revealed it to him.
    D. he could not deny that Jesus was a sinless man.

_____12. What statement did Job make that was advanced far beyond the common beliefs of his day?

    A. The earth pulls on the moon.
    B. The planet Saturn has rings.
    C. The planets revolve around the sun.
    D. The earth hangs on nothing.

_____13. What does archeology confirm about Belshazzar?

    A. the spelling of his name
    B. that a king by this name did rule Babylon
    C. that he conquered the Assyrian empire
    D. the dates of his birth and death

_____14. Two or three centuries ago, skeptics charged that the Bible did not agree with science, history, or geography. The best response to such claims was

    A. to redefine the doctrine of inspiration to allow for such errors in the Bible while keeping the doctrine of salvation intact.
    B. to maintain that either the findings of these sciences can be harmonized with the Bible's teachings or else the critics are wrong.
    C. to remain uncommitted on the doctrine of inerrancy until the critics' charges could be answered.
    D. to discredit the critics by publicizing their evil lifestyles.

Essay

15. Explain why prophecy would be stronger than archeology as an external evidence supporting the divine claims of Scripture.

16. Explain why personal testimony could be a stronger argument than prophecy in proving the Bible's claims.

17. Why are critics so intent on proving that Daniel was written around the second century B.C.?

18. How would you respond to the following statement?

"The fact that many people have found joy and victory through devotion to the Bible is, to me, not a compelling reason for becoming a Christian. Not that I oppose their devotion—it certainly has changed their lives for the better. However, only the weak-minded need such a remedy. Many people are not able to cope with their own addictions or fear of the unknown—particularly their fear of death. Those, on the other hand, that have been adequately educated and properly trained in dealing with life's challenges do not need such 'props' to hold them up mentally and emotionally."

Notes

Photograph Credits

The following agencies and individuals have furnished materials to meet the photographic needs of this textbook. We wish to express our gratitude to them for their important contribution.

American Schools of Oriental Research
Bowen Bible Lands Collection
Consulate General of Israel, NY
Israel Ministry of Tourism
Library of Congress
Marquette Manor Baptist Church
Bryan Smith
Unusual Films

Chapter 1
Unusual Films 6

Chapter 3
Unusual Films 39 (top)

Chapter 4
Bryan Smith 51; Consulate General of Israel, NY 52 (top); Israel Ministry of Tourism 52 (bottom both); Unusual Films 56, 57

Chapter 5
American Schools of Oriental Research 73; Unusual Films, courtesy of Bowen Bible Lands Collection, Bob Jones University 77; photo courtesy of Marquette Manor Baptist Church 78 (top); Unusual Films 78 (bottom); Library of Congress 79